World in Focus

United Kingdom

ALEX WOOLF

WAYLAND

First published in 2006 by Wayland,
an imprint of Hachette Children's Books

© Wayland 2006

Commissioning editor: Victoria Brooker
Editor: Nicola Edwards
Inside design: Chris Halls, www.mindseyedesign.co.uk
Cover design: Wayland

Series concept and project management by EASI-Educational Resourcing
(info@easi-er.co.uk)
Statistical research: Anna Bowden
Maps and graphs: Martin Darlison, Encompass Graphics

British Library Cataloguing in Publication Data
Woolf, Alex
    UK. - (World in focus)
    1. Great Britain - Juvenile literature
    I. Title II. Norcup, Jo
    941'.086

ISBN-10: 0750246839
ISBN-13: 9780750246835

Printed and bound in China

Hachette Children's Books
338 Euston Road, London NW1 3BH

Cover (top): The Great Glen in the Scottish Highlands; (bottom): The Houses of Parliament, London.
Title page: Visitors to the Bullring, Birmingham with the Selfridges building in the background.

Acknowledgements. The author and publisher would like to thank Jo Norcup for her contribution to this publication and
the following for allowing their pictures to be reproduced in it:
Easi-Images (Rob Bowden) cover bottom, title page, 4 , 5, 6, 12, 15, 16, 17, 19, 20, 23, 27, 29, 30, 33, 35, 38, 39, 41, 43, 48, 53,
54, 56, 57, 58; Easi-Images (Adrian Cooper) 44, 55; Corbis 9 (Archivo Iconografico, S.A.),10 (Gianni Dagli Orti), 13
(Bettmann), 18 (London Aerial Photo Library), 21 (Richard Klune), 22 (Nic Bothma/Pool/Reuters), 24 (Yves
Herman/Reuters), 25 (Lewis Alan), 34, 36 (John Kolesidis), 37 (Reuters), 42 (Eleanor Bentall), 46 (Bettmann), 47 (Gideon
Mendel), 49 (Ashley Cooper), 51 (Robert Paterson/Reuters) 59 (Stephen Hird/Reuters); Chris Fairclough Worldwide/Chris
Fairclough cover top, 8, 14, 26, 28, 40, 45, 50; Mary Evans/Margaret Monck Photographs 11; Courtesy of Toyota (GB) Plc
31; Associated Ports' Port of Southampton 32; Edward Parker 52.

The website addresses (URLs) included in this book were valid at the time of
going to press. However, because of the nature of the Internet, it is possible that
some addresses may have changed, or sites may have changed or closed down
since publication. While the author and Publishers regret any inconvenience this
may cause the readers, no responsibility for any such changes can be accepted
by either the author or the Publisher.

The directional arrow portrayed on the map on page 7 provides only an approximation of north.

The data used to produce the graphics and data panels in this title were the latest available at the time of production.

CONTENTS

CHAPTER 1

The United Kingdom – An Overview

The United Kingdom (UK) is a nation on the British Isles of north-western Europe, across the English Channel from continental Europe. It consists of four political divisions – England, Scotland, Wales (which make up the island of Great Britain) and Northern Ireland (the northeastern part of the island of Ireland).

The UK's landscape offers rich variety. Much of Scotland and Wales display rugged and mountainous terrain punctuated by deep valleys, while most of England spreads out in undulating plains cut into a patchwork of fields and meadows. The UK is a land of ancient castles, stately homes and small villages as well as sprawling modern towns and cities.

A GLOBAL PLAYER

During the 19th and early 20th centuries, the UK became the world's biggest economic and military power, when it controlled vast territories around the world (see page 11). The British Empire was the largest the world had ever seen, occupying a quarter of the Earth's land surface and including about a quarter of the human race. The British spread their way of life, language, institutions and traditions throughout their empire.

▼ The Welsh landscape is famous for its sharply rising hills and green valleys. There are three National Parks in Wales, set up to protect the country's scenery and wildlife.

Although it is no longer at the hub of an empire, the UK continues to play a highly influential role in global affairs. As head of the Commonwealth of Nations (an institution made up mostly of former colonies of the British Empire) it has maintained close economic and political relations with many of the countries it once ruled. The UK is one of only five permanent members of the United Nations (UN) Security Council, a founding member of the North Atlantic Treaty Organization (NATO), and a key nation in the European Union (EU).

Britain is also one of the richest countries in the world, with the fourth largest gross national product. By far the largest proportion of its wealth is earned in the service sector, particularly banking, insurance and business services. London, the capital city, is one of the world's leading financial and commercial centres.

▲ London, the UK's capital city, contains a mixture of traditional and modern architecture, from the nineteenth-century Tower Bridge (on the right) to the recently built office blocks seen in the foreground.

NATIONAL CULTURE

Alongside its modern identity, the UK is also a country of deep-rooted traditions with a strong sense of its own history. For example, every year on 5 November, the British people commemorate the foiling of a plot to blow up the British Parliament in 1605. Today, its monarch, though no longer politically powerful, remains an important national figurehead for many Britons, and a highly recognizable symbol of the UK around the world.

Since the 1960s, the UK has also become known worldwide for its popular culture, including

◀ Today, many British cities contain large communities of ethnic minorities. In Birmingham, shown here, around 22 per cent of the population are of Afro-Caribbean or Asian origin.

subcontinent, the Caribbean and West Africa. This migration has added greatly to the UK's ethnic and cultural diversity, enriching all areas of British society, from music and the arts to business and politics.

These developments and many others throughout its history have made the UK the country it is today: outward looking, generally tolerant of other beliefs and cultures, yet also proud of its traditions.

Sometimes, the UK's role in international affairs can lead to problems. For example, the UK's traditionally close ties with the USA can lead to friction with its partners in the European Union – most recently in 2003 with the UK decision to take part in the US-led invasion of Iraq which was strongly opposed by some countries in Europe, including France and Germany.

theatre, film, television and popular music. But perhaps its greatest export has been the English language, now spoken as a first or second language across a large part of the world.

A CHANGING SOCIETY

Throughout its history, the UK has experienced a long succession of invasions and migrations. This trend continued in the second half of the 20th century, when the British government invited people from its former colonies to help with its rebuilding effort following World War II (1939–1945). In response, tens of thousands migrated to Britain from the Indian

Physical geography

- Land area: 241,590 sq km/93,278 sq miles
- Water area: 3,230 sq km/1,247 sq miles
- Total area: 244,820 sq km/94,525 sq miles
- World rank (by area): 79
- Land boundaries: 360 km/224 miles
- Border countries: Ireland
- Coastline: 12,429 km/7,718 miles
- Highest point: Ben Nevis (1,343 m/4,406 ft)
- Lowest point: The Fens (-4 m/-13 ft)

Source: CIA World Factbook

Legend
★ Capital
● Cities > 1,000,000
● Cities > 500,000
● Cities > 200,000
• other cities
▲ Mountain

Orkney Islands

North Sea

Wick

Outer Hebrides

NORTH WEST HIGHLANDS

Isle of Skye

Loch Ness

Inverness

Aberdeen

GRAMPIAN MOUNTAINS

Ben Nevis 1,343m

SCOTLAND

Dundee

ATLANTIC OCEAN

Glasgow   Clyde

Edinburgh

UNITED

SOUTHERN UPLANDS

Shetland Islands

Mainland

N

0   50   100 kilometres
0   50   100 miles

Londonderry

NORTHERN IRELAND

Lough Neagh

Belfast

Carlisle

Newcastle-upon-Tyne

Tyne

Sunderland

North Sea

KINGDOM

Tees

Middlesbrough

LAKE DISTRICT

IRELAND

Isle of Man

Irish Sea

Blackpool

Liverpool

Bradford   Leeds

Bolton   Huddersfield

York

Ouse

Kingston upon Hull

PENNINES

Manchester

Stockport

Sheffield

Stoke-on-Trent

Snowdon 1,085m

ENGLAND

Trent

Derby   Nottingham

Norwich

CAMBRIAN MTNS

Wolverhampton   Walsall

Leicester

THE FENS

Peterborough

Dudley   Birmingham

Coventry

Northampton

Cambridge

Ipswich

Worcester

Cheltenham

Luton

Colchester

WALES

Gloucester   Oxford

Chelmsford

Swansea   Newport

Severn

Swindon

LONDON

Southend-on-Sea

Cardiff

Reading

Thames

Bristol   Bath

Canterbury

Crawley

Dover

ATLANTIC OCEAN

Southampton

Portsmouth

Brighton & Hove

Eastbourne

Exe

Poole

Exeter

Bournemouth

FRANCE

Plymouth

English Channel

Penzance

Channel Islands

Alderney

Guernsey

FRANCE

Jersey

CHAPTER 2

History

For much of its history, the UK has been a target for invasion and settlement by people from many parts of the world. Successive waves of migrants have left their mark on British culture, language and beliefs and helped create the nation of today. In turn, the British have explored, traded with, settled in and dominated other countries around the globe.

ANCIENT BRITAIN

In about 6500 BC the glaciers that covered the British mainland melted, and the land bridge between Britain and France flooded, creating the island of Great Britain. Archaeological evidence reveals that the early inhabitants of Britain comprised a varied group of people who had travelled from the European mainland. The population was small and scattered.

In about 4000 BC, knowledge of agriculture arrived in Britain from Europe, ushering in the New Stone Age, or Neolithic Period. Neolithic people cleared large areas of forest for farmland. They mined flint, made pottery and built Britain's first stone and wooden structures.

Metalworking arrived in Britain between about 3000 and 2500 BC. Bronze tools and weapons gradually replaced flint and copper in about 2000 BC – the start of the Bronze Age. By 1400 BC, Bronze Age people had built many circles of standing stones in Britain, including Stonehenge in Wiltshire. The Iron Age began with the introduction of iron in about 700 BC. Between 500 and 100 BC, a people called the Celts from Central and Western Europe began to settle in Britain.

In 55 BC Roman general Julius Caesar invaded Britain. Caesar's stay was brief, but in AD 43, Roman commander Aulus Plautius successfully invaded, and the Romans took control of most of Britain (approximately the area covered by present-day England and Wales) for the next 400 years. On several occasions during the second and third centuries, the Romans advanced into Scotland, but never succeeded in absorbing it into their empire. The legacy of Roman rule included a road network, towns such as London, Colchester and York, architecture – including Roman baths, such as those at Bath – and the Latin language.

▼ Stonehenge is the most famous prehistoric monument in Britain. It was erected between 3000 and 1600 BC, perhaps as a place of worship.

THE MIDDLE AGES

When the Roman legions withdrew in 410 AD in order to defend against attacks on other parts of the empire, closer to Rome, Britain became vulnerable to attack from other invaders desiring territory and resources. Britons were attacked from the north by a people known as the Picts and from Ireland by a people called the Scots. In the mid-400s, Angles, Jutes and Saxons from Germany invaded, driving native Britons to the western fringes of Britain – Wales and Cornwall. The Anglo-Saxons, as they became known, occupied what would become England and Wales. They established several independent kingdoms.

From 787, Vikings from Scandinavia began a wave of invasions, eventually conquering every kingdom except Wessex in the southwest. In 828, the powerful Wessex king Egbert became the first king of all England. The country did not stay united for long, however. In 830, the kingdom of Mercia in the Midlands reestablished its independence, and it was not until Athelstan's reign (924–939) that England became permanently unified.

In 1066, William, Duke of Normandy (a province of France), conquered England. William installed a new ruling class and introduced Norman systems of law and administration. The king offered land to his barons in exchange for military service in a system known as feudalism. French replaced English as the official language.

Focus on: Magna Carta

Most of the kings who ruled England after the Norman Conquest treated their barons fairly and respected the traditions of feudalism. However, King John (1199–1216) ruled without consulting his barons. He demanded more money and services from them than earlier kings. When John lost a war with France, the barons rebelled, and in 1215 they forced him to sign a document, known as the Magna Carta (Great Charter), which limited royal power and made it clear that even the king was not above the law. Magna Carta was an important step forward in the development of democracy in Britain.

▶ A detail from the Bayeux Tapestry, created to celebrate the Norman victory at the Battle of Hastings in 1066. This was the last time Britain was successfully invaded and conquered by a foreign power.

The Normans continued to rule Britain until the twelfth century when a civil war led to the rise of the Plantagenet dynasty, a powerful French family that ruled Britain from 1154 to 1485.

From 1337 to 1453, England and France fought an intermittent conflict known as the Hundred Years' War over the right to control certain territories in France. England lost most of its French lands and declined into a period of civil war called the Wars of the Roses (1455-1485), when the branches of the Plantagenet dynasty, the houses of York and Lancaster, fought for the English crown (the right to be king).

THE TUDORS AND STUARTS

The Wars of the Roses ended with the defeat of the Yorkist king Richard III by the Lancastrian Henry Tudor, who became Henry VII. Under the rule of his son, Henry VIII, England began to reject Catholicism and Wales was annexed to England (1536–43).

In the later 16th century, England grew as an economic and military power. English explorers, such as Sir Francis Drake, traversed the oceans, and English culture enjoyed a flowering of literature with the works of Shakespeare, Marlowe and Spenser. In 1588,

Philip II of Spain sent a fleet called the Armada to try to conquer England and return it to Catholicism, but it was defeated by the English.

▲ Henry VIII married six times during his reign. He finally succeeded in his desire for a son when his third wife, Jane Seymour, gave birth to Edward in 1536. Henry's most successful heir, however, would be his daughter Elizabeth.

Focus on: The English Reformation

In the early 16th century, a movement began in Europe known as the Protestant Reformation, which rejected the authority of the Pope in Rome. In England, Protestantism was greatly helped by Henry VIII's decision to break with the Catholic Church. Henry did this because his desire for a male heir led him to divorce his wife Catherine and marry his lover, Anne Boleyn – which the Pope would not agree to. By making himself supreme leader of the English Church and removing the Pope's authority in his kingdom, Henry played a major part in the rise of the Protestant Church in England. The English Reformation was completed under the rule of his daughter, Elizabeth I (1558–1603), when Protestantism became the official religion of England.

In the 17th century, a power struggle between the Crown and Parliament culminated in a civil war (1642–1649). Oliver Cromwell, second in command of the Parliamentary forces, defeated the king's forces, and parliament established the republic known as the Commonwealth, which had no monarch. Although the monarchy was restored in 1660, parliament held onto most of its newly won powers. In 1707, the kingdoms of England and Scotland became joined in the Act of Union. The new nation was known thenceforth as Great Britain.

In 1607, James I of England confiscated lands belonging to the Catholic nobility in the north of Ireland (Ulster) and began to encourage Scottish Protestants to settle there. He believed that this 'plantation of Ulster' would prevent future rebellions in Ireland, and gradually win the population over to Protestantism. Over the next ninety years, well over 100,000 Scottish Protestants settled in Ulster, establishing Protestantism as the dominant religion there.

THE 18TH AND 19TH CENTURIES

The 1700s saw the establishment of a more modern system of government in Britain with the rise of political parties and the appointment of a team of ministers, led by a prime minister, to represent the king in parliament. Britain's expanding colonies in India, the Americas and Australia opened up new opportunities for trade. In 1801, Ireland was annexed to Great Britain to form the United Kingdom. Under Queen Victoria (1837–1901), the British Empire reached its height.

▲ Passengers from a British ship disembark in colonial India in 1916.

Focus on: The Industrial Revolution

Between 1740 and 1850, Britain underwent a period of remarkable economic and social transformation known as the Industrial Revolution. Power-driven machines replaced manual labour in many industries, and giant factories replaced homes and workshops as centres of manufacturing. Large numbers of people moved from the country to the towns in search of work. Industrial output reached new heights in the 19th century, and the country became known as 'the workshop of the world'. But rapid industrialization also created an urban underclass who lived and worked in appalling conditions. Pressure for reform from campaigners such as William and Catherine Booth (who tried to improve the working conditions of women), Elizabeth Gaskell (a novelist who wrote about urban poverty) and Robert Owen (a factory reformer) led to a series of laws that improved conditions for many. For example, a series of Factory Acts beginning in 1833 reduced the working hours and improved the working conditions of women and children employed in factories. The Mines Act of 1842 banned employment of women and children underground.

◀ The Iron Bridge, built over the River Severn in Shropshire in 1779, was the world's first iron bridge. The local area, known as Ironbridge Gorge, is regarded as the birthplace of the Industrial Revolution, and is a major centre of Britain's industrial heritage.

LOSS OF EMPIRE

By the early 1900s, Britain was the richest and most powerful nation in the world. However, World War I (1914–18) cost Britain the lives of 750,000 servicemen and severely weakened the UK economy. The war was between the Allies – Britain, France, the USA and others – and the Central Powers, including Germany, Austria-Hungary, the Ottoman Empire and others. Caused mainly by economic and political rivalry, the war was won by the Allies.

From 1910, a movement grew for Irish independence, resisted fiercely by Protestants in the north. This led to a partition of Ireland in 1921, with the south forming the Irish Free State and the northern province of Ulster remaining part of the UK.

Britain played a major part in the Allied victory in World War II (1939–45), but the war devastated the country's economy and left many of its cities in ruins. Lacking the resources to keep control of its colonies, Britain succumbed to increasing demands for independence from India and countries in Africa, the Caribbean and elsewhere. Having lost its empire, Britain sought new global roles as a founder member of NATO (North Atlantic Treaty Organization), an alliance formed to counter the threat of the USSR (Union of Soviet Socialist Republics) during the Cold War (1945–90), and from 1973 as a member of the EEC (European Economic Community, the EU or European Union from 1993).

WELFARE AND DEVOLUTION

At home, the elected Labour government of 1945–51 created a welfare state, including the National Health Service and a social security system that looked after all citizens 'from cradle to grave'. Major industries were nationalized. Under the Conservative governments of 1979–97, government involvement in citizens' lives was reduced and taxes were lowered.

Since 1997, the UK government has devolved (transferred) some of its powers to new assemblies in Scotland and Wales. In Northern Ireland, prolonged, centuries-long conflict between the republicans (supporting a united Ireland) and the loyalists (supporting Northern Ireland remaining as part of the UK) was partly resolved in a 1998 political settlement in which powers were devolved to a Northern Ireland Assembly. This appeared to bring an end to a 30-year campaign of terrorism by the Provisional IRA (Irish Republican Army), a

▲ Prime Minister Winston Churchill (centre) tours the ruins of Coventry Cathedral following a German air raid. Over 30,000 Britons were killed in bomb attacks during 1940 and 1941.

terrorist organization dedicated to the removal of British forces from Northern Ireland and the establishment of a united Ireland. As well as attacking British military and Ulster police targets in Northern Ireland, the IRA set off bombs and carried out kidnappings and assassinations in mainland Britain. In 2005, the IRA announced the end of its armed struggle.

In recent years, Britain has actively supported American foreign policy in the war against terrorism, and joined the United States in military attacks against Afghanistan in 2001–2 and Iraq in 2003. The invasion of Iraq was opposed by many people in Britain, and led to large-scale anti-war demonstrations.

CHAPTER 3

Landscape and Climate

The UK covers an area of 241,950 sq km (93,278 sq miles) of which 3,230 sq km (1,247 sq miles) comprises water in the form of lakes, rivers and streams. For a relatively small country, the UK has a great diversity of landscapes, from the mountains and valleys of Scotland and Wales to the gentle hills and lowlands of England.

THE NORTH

The Scottish Highlands make up most of northern Scotland. Britain's highest mountain, Ben Nevis, at 1,343 m (4,408 feet), is situated there. South of the Scottish Highlands is a gently rolling plain called the Central Lowlands. The Southern Uplands, a region of low, rounded hills, lie south of the Central Lowlands, and mark the border between Scotland and England. The Cambrian Mountains cover most of Wales and include Wales's highest peak, Mount Snowdon, at 1,085 m (3,560 feet). The south of Wales is mostly plateau, cut through by deep river valleys. The north of England is dominated by the Pennines, an upland region known as the 'backbone of England' that stretches from the Scottish border southwards to Sheffield. Northern Ireland's landscape is generally lower but it has a chain of highland peaks known as the Mountains of Mourne.

THE SOUTH

South of the Pennines, the rest of England and eastern Wales is made up of lowlands. These gently rolling plains are occasionally interrupted by low hills and ridges such as the Mendips near Bristol and the South Downs along the south coast between Southampton and Eastbourne. The Fens of East Anglia and the Somerset Levels are particularly low areas, dominated by wetlands and marshes. The land

◀ The Great Glen in the Scottish Highlands. Formed millions of years ago, this rugged valley is 117 km (73 miles) long and contains three freshwater lakes.

here is very fertile and as a result a large proportion of wetland has been drained to create farmland.

RIVERS

Many of the UK's rivers have wide mouths called estuaries up which ocean tides flow. These include the Thames, Mersey, Humber, Severn, Clyde and Forth. The estuaries provide excellent harbours, and the cities on these rivers are all important ports. These include London (Thames), Bristol (Severn) and Glasgow (Clyde).

▲ Liverpool's so-called Three Graces – the Royal Liver Building, the Cunard Building and Customs House – seen from a ferry on the River Mersey.

COASTS AND ISLANDS

The UK's highly varied coastline includes cliffs, mudflats, rocky beaches, salt marshes, sand dunes, sandy beaches and fishing towns nestling in sheltered bays. Off Britain's coasts are a number of small islands which are all part of the UK. These include Anglesey, off the

Did you know?

The lowest point in the island of Great Britain is in the Fens, near Ely. It ranges from sea level to 4 m (13 feet) below sea level, depending on the tide of the North Sea.

Did you know?

The UK's largest lake is Lough Neagh in Northern Ireland. It is about 29 km (18 miles) long and 24 km (15 miles) wide at its widest point, and covers about 388 sq km (150 sq miles).

northwest coast of Wales; the Isle of Wight, off England's southern coast; the Outer Hebrides, an archipelago of islands off the west coast of Scotland; the Orkney Islands to the north-east of Scotland; and the Shetland Islands, about 100 miles north of Scotland. The UK also has several dependencies close to its shores, including the Isle of Man in the Irish Sea and the Channel Islands off the northern coast of France. These dependencies are not part of the UK, but have a very close relationship with it.

A TEMPERATE CLIMATE

The UK has a mild climate, influenced by wind and ocean currents, which help to prevent extremes of heat and cold that may be experienced by other places of a similar latitude, such as Labrador in North America. The main

cause of the UK's mild temperatures is the Gulf Stream, a warm ocean current that sweeps up from the equator and flows past the British Isles. South-westerly winds blow across this current and keep winter temperatures around 10°C (18°F) higher than they would otherwise be. As a result, winter temperatures seldom drop lower than -12°C (10°F).

In the summer, the ocean is cooler than the land, and winds blowing in from the sea prevent high temperatures on land, which rarely exceed 90°F (32°C). Scotland and northern England are generally cooler than the UK average, and can be affected by cool Arctic air from the North Pole. The south-east of England is generally warmer than the rest of England and benefits from warm continental air travelling north from mainland Europe.

A LAND OF RAIN

The sea winds also bring plenty of rain. In general, western regions are considerably wetter than eastern areas. Highland areas are also wetter than lowlands, and above 600 m (2,000 feet), average annual precipitation is around 1,500 mm (60 inches) and can be as high as 5,100 mm (200 inches). This compares to a UK average of around 1,000 mm (40 inches). The driest area is south-eastern England, parts of which receive less than 510 mm (20 inches) per year. The rain generally falls as a light, steady drizzle, and is fairly evenly distributed through the year, giving Britain the reputation as a land of seemingly constant rainfall.

◀ Holidaymakers on the beach at the resort town of Blackpool in Lancashire. Above them, the famous Blackpool Tower soars to a height of 158 metres (518 feet).

Focus On: Climate Change

The 1990s was the warmest and driest decade in the UK since records began in 1860. Experts have warned that this may be evidence of climate change caused by increased carbon dioxide emissions due to human consumption of fossil fuels. In the UK, climate change is expected to increase average temperatures by 1 – 4.5°C (1.8°–8.1°F) by 2100, with the greatest changes felt in the south of England. Rainfall patterns are also expected to change, with drier summers and wetter winters. In the south of England, precipitation may be reduced by up to 50 per cent, forcing farmers to consider growing crops more suited to a Mediterranean climate, such as grapes and peppers. Winter storms are also likely to increase, and flooding could become a regular problem for up to two million people in the UK by 2050.

▲ The Thames flood barrier, completed in 1984, is designed to protect London from flooding. During storms or high tides, massive steel gates are raised from the river bed, forming a wall across the river.

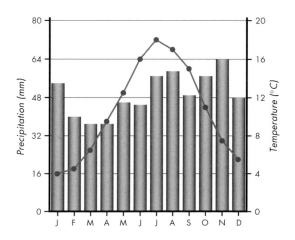

▲ Average monthly climate conditions in London.

CHAPTER 4

Population and Settlements

For its size, the UK supports a large population. In 2005 the population stood at 49.4 million, giving the UK a population density of around 242 people per sq km (628 per sq mile). This is more than double the population density of France and nearly eight times that of the USA.

AN URBAN NATION

The landscape has influenced where people have settled. A large majority of the population (84 per cent) live on the generally flatter and larger landmass of England. Scotland is home to eight per cent of British people, while a further five per cent and three per cent live in Wales and Northern Ireland respectively.

The British are also a largely urban people, with 89 per cent living in towns and cities.

About one third of British people live in one of England's seven metropolitan areas. These are Greater London, Greater Manchester, Merseyside, South Yorkshire, Tyne and Wear, West Midlands and West Yorkshire. The largest cities are London (7.6 million), Birmingham and Manchester (both 2.2 million), and Leeds (1.4 million).

AN AGEING POPULATION

People in the UK are, on average, living longer, studying longer, marrying later and having fewer children than previous generations. These social trends, combined with improvements in healthcare and education, have given the UK a declining and ageing population. The proportion of young people (0-14 years), for example, fell from 23.3 per cent of the

▶ An aerial view of a residential area of Birmingham in the West Midlands. Like many British cities, Birmingham's population expanded rapidly in the twentieth century, and it is now the UK's second largest city.

population in 1960 to 18.1 per cent in 2003. Over the same time period, the proportion of the population above retirement age (65 years) increased from 11.7 per cent to 16 per cent. If this trend continues it is likely to lead to social problems, as taxes will need to increase to pay for the larger numbers of retired people. There are implications for the pensions industry: it has been estimated that 12 million people in the UK are not saving enough towards their retirement. To address this, the government plans to increase the retirement age from 60 to 65.

▼ Elderly women enjoying a day out at Norwich Cathedral. With rising numbers of people over the age of 65, the 'grey pound' (the spending power of retired people) has become a significant force in the UK economy.

Focus on: London

The capital city of the UK is one of the world's oldest cities. It began as two cities – the City of London, founded by the Romans in AD 43, and the City of Westminster, established about 1,000 years later. Today, Greater London is the UK's most urbanized area. With 7.6 million residents, it contains about an eighth of the UK's entire population and has the largest population of any city in Europe. A significant factor in the city's growth is immigration. Always a cosmopolitan city, it has attracted people from many parts of the Commonwealth and elsewhere so that today nearly one third of London's population come from overseas. This has helped to give the city a rich and diverse culture.

ETHNIC DIVERSITY

Since the 1950s, the population of the UK has become increasingly multi-ethnic. However, this trend should not be exaggerated. According to the UK census (2001), ethnic minority groups accounted for less than six per cent of the total population. The largest ethnic minorities are those originating from the Caribbean and Africa (875,000 people), India (840,255 people), and Pakistan and Bangladesh (639,390 people). There are also substantial numbers of Americans, Australians and Chinese, as well as Europeans. The UK's immigrant population is to be found mostly concentrated in inner-city areas, and more than half live in Greater London.

CITY AND COUNTRY

Since the 1950s, many of the UK's inner cities (the central parts of cities), which rose to greatness during the Industrial Revolution, have been in decline. Problems include a lack of jobs, poor housing and rising crime. Inner-city populations have fallen as people have moved out to the suburbs. Advances in transportation have made it much easier for people to live in the suburbs and work in the city.

In 1988, the government launched a campaign to revive inner cities. 'Enterprise Zones' were established in cities such as Cardiff, Belfast, Glasgow and Liverpool where tax incentives were offered to new businesses willing to invest. Some regeneration schemes have improved inner-city life, although there are still many deprived and crime-ridden neighbourhoods.

? Did you know?

Migration may be crucial to the UK's future prosperity. The combined effects of emigration from the UK, a declining birth rate and increased longevity, mean that by 2025, 10 million migrants of working age will be needed if the UK is to sustain its current levels of wealth and productivity.

► A street festival in Stoke on Trent in the West Midlands celebrates the multicultural nature of the region. The largest ethnic minority populations in the West Midlands originate from India, Pakistan and the Caribbean.

The exodus from the inner cities has changed the complexion of the UK's rural communities, which were once dominated by farming. Many villages now contain more commuters than full-time farmers. The countryside has also proved attractive to retired city workers, and in places like Cornwall, Devon, East and West Sussex, and parts of Wales, more than a fifth of the population is over retirement age. In recent decades, the beauty and variety of the English countryside has proved a magnet for tourists, and many residents of rural communities now work in the tourist industry.

HOUSING

In recent years, various social trends have led to housing shortages in parts of the UK. Increasing divorce rates and a greater number of single-person households have caused a rise in single-occupancy housing from 14 per cent in 1961 to 29 per cent in 2001. Another trend has been the

disproportionately high demand for housing in London and the south-east, due to the increasing number of jobs in this region. In London alone, the demand for housing grows by an estimated 90,000 every year.

▲ Newcastle, in the north-east of England, has enjoyed substantial redevelopment of its Quayside. This formerly declining inner city area is becoming a major centre of tourism and leisure.

Population data

- Population: 59.4 million
- Population 0-14 yrs: 18%
- Population 15-64 yrs: 66%
- Population 65+ yrs: 16%
- Population growth rate: 0.3%
- Population density: 242.6 per sq km/ 628.4 per sq mile
- Urban population: 89%
- Major cities: London 7,615,000
  Birmingham 2,215,000
  Manchester 2,193,000

Source: United Nations and World Bank

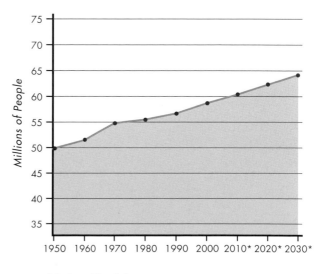

* Projected Population

▲ Population growth 1950-2030

CHAPTER 5

Government and Politics

The UK is a constitutional monarchy, which means that the head of state is the king or queen, ruling to the extent allowed by the various documents and customs that make up its constitution. In fact, since the early 18th century, the monarch's role has been largely ceremonial, and political power actually rests with the prime minister and the cabinet. The prime minister is a member of parliament (MP) and the leader of the largest political party in the House of Commons, which is the elected chamber of parliament. The cabinet is made up of MPs from the majority party, appointed by the prime minister to head the various departments of state, such as the Treasury and the Home Office.

PARLIAMENT

The prime minister and the cabinet initiate policy. However, only parliament has the power to make new laws. The UK parliament is made up of two chambers, the House of Commons and the House of Lords. The House of Commons is composed of elected MPs, each of which represents a constituency in the country. The House of Lords is made up of peers who have either inherited their position or been appointed to it. The House of Commons is the

▼ Queen Elizabeth II on a visit to Nigeria in 2003. One of the Queen's roles as head of state is to represent Britain on state visits to other countries and on ceremonial occasions.

more powerful of the two chambers, and since 1911 the House of Lords has only had the power to delay legislation.

THE ELECTORAL SYSTEM

Since the late 17th century the UK has had a two-party system. Since the 1920s, the dominant parties have been the Conservative and Labour parties. Smaller parties such as the Liberal Democrats and Scottish and Welsh nationalist parties have only managed to gain relatively limited representation in parliament. This is because the electoral system that operates in the UK, known as 'first-past-the-post', tends to favour larger parties. Under this

▲ The Houses of Parliament in London. Here, members of the House of Commons and House and Lords debate and pass the laws that govern the UK.

system, candidates with the most votes win, and there are no prizes for coming second. There have been calls by organizations such as the Electoral Reform Society and the Liberal Democratic Party to reform the UK electoral system so that it more fairly reflects actual voting patterns across the country. However, first-past-the-post does have the advantage, according to its supporters, of producing firm and decisive government.

Focus on: The UK's 'Unwritten Constitution'

A constitution is a set of rules that govern a country's political behaviour. British government evolved in a rather haphazard way over many centuries, and as a result its constitution is not a clear set of rules laid down in a single document, as in France or the USA. Instead, the British constitution is to be found in a range of historical customs, laws and conventions.

DEVOLUTION

In 1999, the UK government handed over certain powers to newly set up national assemblies in the UK's regions – Scotland, Wales and Northern Ireland. The Scottish Parliament has powers over areas such as education, health, housing, transport, the environment and agriculture, while central government retains control of foreign affairs, defence and economic policy. The Welsh assembly is much less powerful than the Scottish Parliament since it lacks the power to make new laws or gather taxes. The Northern Ireland assembly was granted limited executive and legislative powers but was dissolved in 2002 following a breakdown in the peace process, and direct rule from the UK was reimposed.

LOCAL GOVERNMENT

Most everyday services in the UK are controlled and maintained by local authorities. These include roads, parks, libraries, schools, street cleaning, fire fighting, social services and rubbish collection. Local governments have few law-making powers and must act within the laws laid down by parliament, but they do have the power to raise property taxes, which amount to about a quarter of all the tax revenues raised in the UK.

assembly, with responsibility for public transport, policing, emergency services, the environment and planning. If the office of mayor is seen as a success, other UK cities may also get the chance to elect their own mayor.

THE EUROPEAN UNION

The UK's membership of the EU has been a cause of controversy in recent years. The EU began as the EEC (see page 13), an alliance of European nations to promote free trade in Europe. However, it has since developed powerful institutions of its own such as the European Parliament and a Court of Justice. It also has its own economic and social policy and the beginnings of a foreign policy. The EU

Most cities are run by metropolitan councils made up of elected members. London has its own separate structure of government, with 32 boroughs. In 2000, London gained its first directly elected mayor, together with an elected

▲ UK Prime Minister Tony Blair (centre) meets with the presidents of the European Union and European Parliament at a summit of EU heads of state. Many Britons remain sceptical about the benefits of closer integration with other European states.

is beginning to resemble a state in its own right, and the UK, like other member nations, is obliged to accept the EU's decisions. Many in the UK fear that these developments threaten the sovereignty (authority) of the UK parliament.

 Did you know?

There are a total of 468 local authorities in the UK and 26,000 elected councillors. Over two million people are employed in local government in the UK.

Focus on: Northern Ireland

In 1922, when Ireland gained its independence from the UK, six of the northern counties, known collectively as Northern Ireland or Ulster, decided to remain a part of the UK. The people of Northern Ireland have long been divided on political and religious lines. The majority are Protestants. Most of these are unionists and wish to remain a part of the UK. A large minority of the population are Catholic (as are most of the people in the Republic of Ireland to the south). Most Catholics are nationalists, or Republicans, and support the reunification of Ireland. Conflict between the unionists and nationalists broke out in the late 1960s. A peace process began in 1994, leading in 1998 to a peace agreement. A power-sharing legislature called the Northern Ireland Assembly was established in 1999. But continued political conflict led the British government to suspend the assembly. In 2005, the Republican terrorist group, the IRA, agreed to end the armed struggle and support the political process, and the UK government responded by reducing the number of troops it had stationed in Northern Ireland.

▶ Riot police take cover as unionist protesters throw missiles and set a roadblock on fire in Belfast in July 2000. Despite progress towards peace, a simmering mistrust remains between the two communities in Northern Ireland, which can sometimes explode into violence.

CHAPTER 6

Energy and Resources

The UK has larger energy resources – including coal, oil and natural gas – than any other member of the EU. It has plenty of good agricultural land and forests and is one of Europe's leading fishing nations. The UK also benefits from reasonable reserves of minerals.

FOSSIL FUELS

The UK coal industry has been in steady decline for the past 100 years. Since its peak year of 1913 when 300 million tons (305 million tonnes) were produced, output has fallen by more than 80 per cent. During the 1980s, many coal mines were closed because they were no longer economic and it was cheaper to import energy resources from other countries.

The discovery of oil in the North Sea in the 1960s and its subsequent exploitation from the mid-1970s have greatly boosted Britain's energy supplies. The UK's North Sea oilfields produce an average output of nearly three million barrels per day.

Natural gas from the North Sea began to be available in large quantities from 1967. A national network of pipelines has been built, and in 2001 it contributed towards 40 per cent of the UK's total energy consumption, compared to 32 per cent from oil and 17 per cent from coal. Estimates suggest the North Sea reserves of oil and gas are likely to start running low between 2020 and 2030. Long before then, the UK will need to start importing these resources in larger quantities to fulfill the UK's energy requirements.

ALTERNATIVE ENERGY SOURCES

The burning of fossil fuels (coal, oil and gas) causes carbon dioxide emissions, which pollute the atmosphere and add to global warming. These fuels are also not renewable. Using fossil fuels is therefore not a sustainable policy in the long term, and alternatives must be found. In 1997, the UK signed up to the Kyoto Protocol,

◀ An oil rig in the North Sea. Production of North Sea oil has declined steadily since its peak in 1999.

an international agreement which commits it to reducing carbon dioxide emissions by cutting down on energy consumption and looking at alternative energy sources.

One alternative is nuclear energy. The UK has 12 nuclear power stations which together supply around 23 per cent of the country's electricity. However, nuclear energy also has its drawbacks: an accident at a nuclear plant can cause a major environmental disaster and the waste produced is very dangerous, difficult to dispose of, and, even when carefully disposed of, remains dangerously radioactive for thousands of years.

▲ There are currently 136 wind farms in the UK, with plans to build many more. Although a source of renewable energy, critics complain that they are noisy and spoil the look of the natural environment.

? Did you know?

The world's first large-scale nuclear power station was opened in 1956 at Calder Hall, Cumbria in north-west England.

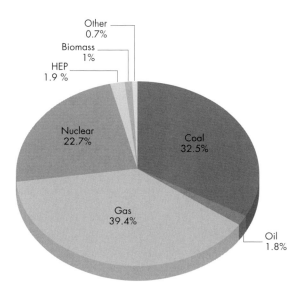

▲ Electricity production by type

Other 0.7%
Biomass 1%
HEP 1.9 %
Nuclear 22.7%
Coal 32.5%
Gas 39.4%
Oil 1.8%

Energy data

📂 Energy consumption as % of world total: 2.4
📂 Energy consumption by sector (% of total):

Industry:	26.1
Transportation:	32.3
Agriculture:	0.8
Services:	10.5
Residential:	26.6
Other:	3.7

📂 CO_2 emissions as % of world total: 2.3
📂 CO_2 emissions per capita in tonnes p.a.: 9.0

Source: World Resources Institute

There are also non-polluting, renewable energy sources, such as biomass (any organic material that can be converted into a source of energy), wind, wave, tidal and solar power. In 2005, approximately 3.6 per cent of electricity in the UK came from renewable sources. The government has given targets to electricity suppliers to increase the percentage of electricity they supply from renewable sources to 10.4 per cent by 2011.

AGRICULTURE AND FORESTRY

Approximately 75 per cent of UK land is used for agriculture. The most important crops are wheat, barley, oats, sugar beets, potatoes and rapeseed, which is used to make vegetable oil, livestock feed and industrial lubricant. The main kinds of livestock are cattle, sheep, pigs and poultry. The UK imports about a third of its food supply. Imports include bananas, citrus fruits, peppers, pineapples, sugar and other foods that cannot easily be grown in the UK's climate. As a member of the EU, UK agricultural policy conforms to the EU's Common Agricultural Policy (CAP). The CAP offers farmers a stable income by providing a system of minimum prices for their products and offering subsidies so that their goods are competitive on world markets. British governments have criticized the CAP because UK farmers receive less financial help from the CAP than British taxpayers pay into it (because the UK has a smaller farming sector than other European countries). Many in the UK feel that their taxes are supporting inefficient European farmers.

About 10 per cent of UK land is devoted to forestry. British forests produce nearly 9 million cubic metres (30 million cubic feet) of wood

◀ Jersey cows at a dairy farm in Hampshire. The number of dairy farms in the UK fell by 46 per cent between 1985 and 2003. Dairy farmers are finding it increasingly difficult to make a profit from milk production.

each year. However, this provides the country with only about 15 per cent of its annual timber requirements. Most of the UK's imported wood comes from producers in Europe and North and South America.

FISHING

Being surrounded by sea, fishing has naturally always been important to the people of the UK. The most popular local fish are cod, haddock, mackerel, herring, whiting and plaice, as well as various kinds of shellfish. Fish farms produce salmon, trout and shellfish. In total, the UK fishing industry catches around 840,000 tons (853,000 tonnes) of fish annually. However, the industry has been in decline for some years due to overfishing, resulting in depleted fish stocks, especially of cod. Under EU rules, the UK has had to limit the amount of fish it can catch within British waters, as these seas are also fished by other member states. The UK fishing industry now supplies only about half the nation's total demand.

MINERALS

Metals mined in the UK include tin and zinc. However, its most valuable minerals are non-metallic, and include sand, gravel and limestone, which are quarried for use in the construction industry. Chalk, used for making cement, is found in large quantities in south-east England. Other minerals include dolomite, slate, barite, talc, celestite, sandstone, gypsum and various types of clay. The south-west peninsula is known for its kaolin, or china clay, used to make pottery.

Focus on: Water Resources

Despite receiving plenty of rainfall, the UK has fairly limited water resources and frequently faces water shortages, particularly during the summer months. Summer rainfall does not help the water supply because the ground is too hard to absorb the rain and refill the reservoirs. Winter rain is often so heavy that it does not soak into rock, but saturates the topsoil and then runs off into rivers. For its size, the UK is also a big consumer of water, at 150 litres per person per day. Another problem is water leakage. An estimated three billion litres of water are lost each day through broken and leaking pipes.

▲ During dry spells in the summer months, water levels in British reservoirs can often sink dangerously low.

CHAPTER 7

Economy and Income

The UK is one of the world's leading economies with the fourth largest gross national product. However, its economy took a long time to recover from the devastating effects of World War II, and it was not until the 1990s that it showed significant improvement. The economy was helped partly by membership of the EEC (later, EU), which it joined in 1973. Today, more than half of the UK's trade in goods is with other members of the EU.

Between 1995 and 2005, the UK economy grew at a faster rate than many other top industrial nations. Unemployment and inflation both remained low, in stark contrast to the 1970s and 1980s. London's role as a global financial centre has helped greatly, as has the fact that American and Japanese companies frequently choose the UK as a European base for their factories and offices.

MANUFACTURING

During the 1970s British manufacturing declined in productivity and competitiveness. In the following decade, the Conservative government privatized the UK's heavy industries, including car and truck production, aircraft building and steel production. This improved profitability at the expense of jobs and output. Today, the UK's manufacturing sector amounts to just 20 per cent of the national economy, compared to about 40 per cent in 1945. It generates over 150 billion pounds per year and employs four million people, or around 14 per cent of the workforce.

The UK's most significant manufacturing industries are engineering, food and drink, tobacco, chemicals, paper and printing, metals and minerals, clothing and footwear. The fastest-growing industries are pharmaceuticals and electrical engineering.

◀ Since the 1980s, London's Docklands area has been transformed into a major financial centre, with many of the world's banks opening offices there.

▲ A production line worker at a factory near Derby owned by the Japanese car manufacturer Toyota. Investment by foreign companies has boosted employment in a number of UK regions.

 Did you know?

London has more foreign banks located there than any other city in the world.

Economic data

☞ Gross National Income (GNI) in US$: 2,016,393,000,000

☞ World rank by GNI: 4

☞ GNI per capita in US$: 33,940

☞ World rank by GNI per capita: 13

☞ Economic growth: 2.0%

Source: World Bank

Focus on: Liverpool

With its large port and its location in north-west England, the city of Liverpool played a key role in the growth of UK trade with the Americas and the West Indies in the 18th century. The city expanded to become the centre of the UK's shipping industry in the 19th century, with 11 km (7 miles) of docks. But by the mid-20th century, Liverpool faced decline as Britain's colonial power faded and it struggled to recover from two world wars. Under-investment made matters worse, and thousands of dock workers found themselves unemployed. In the 2000s, the city's economic life was revived thanks to tourism and a city-centre regeneration scheme. In 2003, Liverpudlians celebrated as their city was named the European Capital of Culture for 2008.

◀ Container ships being loaded with goods at the port of Southampton on the south coast of England. Around 55,000 UK companies export their products around the world.

THE SERVICE SECTOR

In contrast to manufacturing, the UK's service sector has flourished since the 1980s. Today, service industries contribute around 72 per cent to the national economy and employ about 75 per cent of the workforce. The areas of greatest growth are banking, insurance and business support (which includes computing, advertising and market research). With its many historic buildings, picturesque countryside, theatres and museums, the UK also has a thriving tourist industry. Every year about 24 million tourists visit the UK, spending over 10 billion pounds (17 billion dollars).

TRADE

The UK economy has long been dependent on trade with foreign nations. Its farms only produce two-thirds of the food needed to feed its population, and it also must import many of the raw materials it needs for its manufacturing. The total value of the UK's foreign trade (imports and exports) is nearly half the nation's gross domestic product. (The equivalent figure for the USA is just one fifth.) Major UK exports include machinery, cars, electronic equipment, chemicals, oil and financial services.

Half of all UK trade is with EU countries, although its single largest export market and second largest supplier is the USA. Its largest supplier and second largest export market is Germany. Since 1985 (apart from a brief period in the late 1990s) the UK has had a balance of trade deficit, meaning that it imports more goods than it exports.

 Did you know?

UK employers are not allowed to make their staff work longer than 48 hours per week. However, the UK still has one of the longest working weeks in Europe. Employees in France and Spain don't have to work longer than 38 to 40 hours per week.

THE WORKFORCE

There are about 30 million people working in the UK today – about half the total population. A small but growing proportion of these (13 per cent in 2004) are self-employed. A fifth of self-employed people in the UK work in construction. Most others work in sales, catering, finance or insurance.

Today, women account for 47 per cent of the workforce, compared to 32 per cent in 1959. This reflects the changing role of women in the UK, with far more pursuing careers than in the 1950s. However, men and women still generally work in different fields, with about a quarter of women doing administrative or secretarial work, while men are more likely to be managers or working in skilled trades.

THE NORTH-SOUTH DIVIDE

The availability of jobs is not evenly distributed around the UK. People living in the south are likely to be better educated and earn more than those in the north. In 2004, the average weekly wage in the north-east of England was £373 ($654), compared to £451 ($791) in the south-east (although admittedly prices are also higher in the

south-east). Between 1991 and 2001, the UK experienced a large migration of skilled workers, with half a million moving from north to south because of greater job opportunities in southern Britain, especially in London. Over 1.7 million jobs were created in London's financial sector during this period, while the northern cities of Glasgow, Liverpool and Manchester suffered population declines of 8–10 per cent.

▲ Properties for sale in fashionable Brighton, on England's south coast.

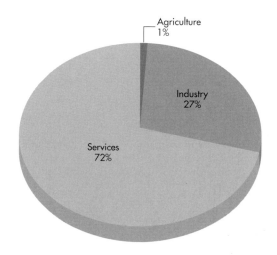

▲ Economy by sector

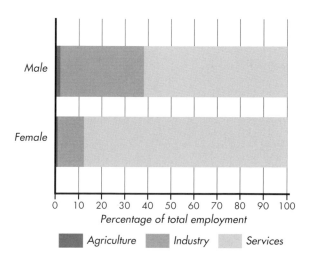

Percentage of total employment

Agriculture   Industry   Services

▲ Labour force by sector and gender

CHAPTER 8

Global Connections

As an island nation with a strong seafaring tradition, the United Kingdom has always had an international outlook. Helped by its historical and cultural ties with the former colonies of its empire, and by its proximity to continental Europe, the UK remains a major global player and influential member of several leading international organizations.

During its imperial heyday, the UK influenced its colonies in many ways, introducing British systems of administration, law and education, as well as British customs and sports. Perhaps the most important legacy of the British Empire is the English language, which today is spoken by about 380 million people as a first language, and is the most widely learned second language in the world. It is also the global 'lingua franca', or common language used to conduct business.

THE COMMONWEALTH

After the British Empire began to fall apart in the first half of the 20th century, a Commonwealth was established consisting of the UK and many of its former colonies. (Two of its members – Cameroon and Mozambique – were not former colonies.) The Commonwealth has 53 member states, and although the British monarch remains its formal head, all its members are politically independent of the UK. The heads of government of the member states meet every two years to discuss matters of common interest.

The aims of the Commonwealth are to promote democracy, good government, human rights and economic development. For example, in the 1980s the Commonwealth imposed political and moral sanctions on apartheid South Africa. This was one

▶ The opening ceremony at the 2002 Commonwealth Games in Manchester. The role of these games, held every four years, is to strengthen the bonds between member nations and encourage sport and physical recreation throughout the Commonwealth.

of several factors that helped to bring about the end of apartheid in the early 1990s. In 2002, the Commonwealth suspended Zimbabwe because of the violence and intimidation of the Zimbabwean government against some of its own people. Admittedly, this action has yet to effect any positive change in Zimbabwe.

GROUP OF EIGHT

The UK is a member of the Group of Eight (or G8), an organization of the eight major industrialized democracies. The UK government has an opportunity to air its views and try to reach international agreement on a range of economic and political issues at the annual G8 summit conference. Topics for debate include arms control, economic development, international terrorism and world health. The 2005 G8 summit, held at Gleneagles, north of Edinburgh in Scotland, resulted in some important agreements covering development in Africa and tackling climate change.

▲ Floral tributes left near the scene of one of the terrorist bomb attacks on London, which occurred on 7 July 2005. The attacks were timed to coincide with the G8 summit.

Focus on: Hong Kong

In 1898, China leased the island of Hong Kong, on its southern coast, to the UK for 99 years. In 1997, as demanded by the terms of the lease, the UK handed back control of the island to China. Many residents of Hong Kong were concerned that China, with its communist policies, would wish to change the island's free-enterprise economy. However, China has allowed Hong Kong to continue with its capitalist economic system and granted it some political autonomy.

Focus on: Overseas Territories

Remnants of the once-mighty British Empire remain in the form of UK overseas territories (formerly known as dependent territories). These include the Falkland Islands, Montserrat, Gibraltar, the Cayman Islands, the Pitcairn Islands and the British Virgin Islands. Most overseas territories were at one time directly administered by officials appointed by the British government. Today, however, most are self-governing colonies, with their own legislatures, only depending on the UK for defence, foreign affairs and some trade issues.

THE EUROPEAN UNION

Since 1973, the UK has been a member of the EU (formerly the EEC until 1993). Being part of this single market with Europe – the largest single market in the world – has greatly benefited the UK economy. It has also given UK citizens the right to travel and work throughout Europe. EU membership gives the UK the opportunity to act in concert with other European nations on matters of international concern such as crime, terrorism, immigration and environmental protection.

On the other hand, the UK's geographical position as an island on the edge of continental Europe and its historic rivalry with several European nations have served to give it a slightly distanced relationship with the EU. The UK decided not to join 12 other EU members in adopting a single currency, the Euro, in 2000, and many in the UK distrust the growing power of the EU to make decisions that affect the lives of British people. For example, European Union directives have made the use of metric weights and measures compulsory throughout the EU. This has caused some anger among traders and members of the public in Britain, where traditional imperial measures are still widely used.

THE UNITED NATIONS

Founded in 1945, the UN is an organization that works for world peace and security. The UK is one of only five permanent members of the UN Security Council. The other four are the USA, France, Russia and China. This body has the power to decide what action the UN should take in order to solve international conflicts. The UK was the first of the permanent members to make its armed forces and police available to the UN for peacekeeping operations, and it has since played a major role in UN operations around the globe, for example, there are nearly 400 British troops in the UN peacekeeping force in Cyprus.

▶ A British member of the UN peacekeeping force helps to guard the buffer zone between the Turkish and Greek communities on the island of Cyprus.

NATO

The UK was a founding member of NATO (see page 13), a military alliance of 20 nations in North America and Europe. It was originally established in 1949 during the Cold War with the USSR and its allies (1945–1990). Since the end of the Cold War, NATO's main roles have been resolving conflicts, peacekeeping and fighting terrorism. In the early 21st century, the UK was involved in all four of NATO's major operations. These involved security operations in Afghanistan, Iraq and the Balkans, and an anti-terrorist operation in the Mediterranean called Operation Active Endeavour which began in 2001 and is still continuing.

Focus on: The Special Relationship

Since joining forces to defeat the Nazis and Fascists in World War II, the UK and USA have been very close political allies. Their shared cultural heritage has generally given the two countries a similar outlook on world events, and the UK has been traditionally very supportive of the USA. This 'special relationship' with the world's only superpower has been very advantageous to the UK. However, it does sometimes cause problems, for example when the British government supported the 2003 US-led invasion of Iraq, which provoked great popular opposition in Britain.

▲ US President George W. Bush (left) at a press conference with Tony Blair, the British Prime Minister.

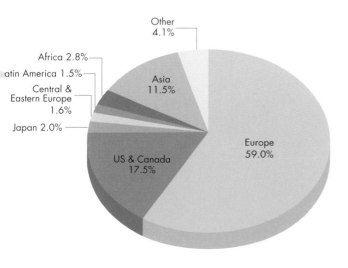

Other 4.1%
Africa 2.8%
Latin America 1.5%
Central & Eastern Europe 1.6%
Japan 2.0%
Asia 11.5%
Europe 59.0%
US & Canada 17.5%

▲ Destination of UK exports by major trading region

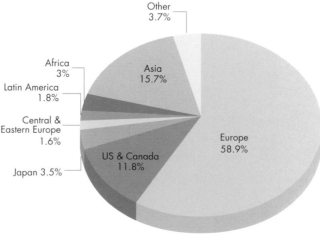

Other 3.7%
Africa 3%
Latin America 1.8%
Central & Eastern Europe 1.6%
Japan 3.5%
Asia 15.7%
Europe 58.9%
US & Canada 11.8%

▲ Origin of UK imports by major trading region

CHAPTER 9

Transport and Communications

Historically, the UK led the world in the development of various forms of transport, including shipping, rail and aviation. Today, the dominant mode of transportation in the UK is the car.

SHIPPING

The UK has long had a significant shipping industry. The irregular coastline of the British Isles provides it with plenty of natural harbours, and there are also many navigable rivers (see page 15). The UK has a large merchant fleet carrying freight to and from the nation's 80 commercial ports, while passenger ships regularly ferry people to and from the European mainland and Ireland. The UK also has a network of inland waterways used to transport goods and for recreational boating.

▼ Private toll roads, such as the M6 toll road in the West Midlands, attempt to combat road congestion.

ROADS

For its size, the UK has a large road network, with around 393,000 km (244,000 miles) of roads, including 3,400 km (2,113 miles) of motorways. Road transport is by far the most common form of travel in the UK today. About 65 per cent of freight is carried on roads, and about 90 per cent of all passenger travel is by road, and most of that is by private car. The growth in private car ownership is one of the most significant developments in the UK's recent transport history. Between 1980 and 2004 the number of private vehicles increased by 41 per cent. Today, 74 per cent of UK households own at least one car and pay a tax on each vehicle. Road traffic increased by 71 per cent between 1980 and 2000. There is continuous pressure from motorists' pressure groups on the government to build more motorways, especially in the south-east. Government concerns about the road congestion and pollution caused by excessive car use has led them to try to tempt more people to use public transport by raising taxes on fuel. Between 1975 and 2000, fuel tax revenues rose by almost £24 billion, making UK petrol the most expensive in Europe. However, fuel tax protests in 2000 dissuaded the government from implementing any further increases since then.

▲ Trams in the centre of Nottingham – the latest of seven UK cities that have introduced tram systems since 1980, to cope with congestion. Trams run on rails and are powered by electricity from overhead wires.

RAILWAYS

In the 19th century, the UK developed the world's first rail network. From the mid-1950s, a modernization program began and steam trains were replaced by diesel and electric ones. In the late 1960s, competition from the roads began to take effect, and many less profitable branch lines were closed. In the early 21st century, the number of passenger journeys once again approached the levels of the 1950s, although rail had a far smaller share of overall travel. As part of the government's policy to boost train use, there has been significant investment in the West Coast Main Line, which runs between London and Glasgow, with diverging routes to many other British towns and cities. The West Coast Route Modernization programme will involve renewal and modernization of some 1,660 miles of track, including around 10,000 bridges and 2,800 signals.

Focus on: The Channel Tunnel

In 1994, the UK was linked to mainland Europe – for the first time since the Ice Age – by a rail tunnel built underneath the English Channel. The Channel Tunnel is 50 km (31 miles) in length and runs from Folkestone, England, to Calais, France, at an average depth of 40 m (131 feet) below the sea bed. By 2000, the tunnel's trains were carrying half the car traffic between Dover or Folkstone and Calais.

 Did you know?

Today's UK rail network includes 17,274 km (10,734 miles) of railway track, over 2,500 stations and 40,000 bridges and tunnels.

Several British cities have their own rail networks. The largest is the London Underground – the oldest underground railway in the world. Today, London Underground has 408 km (253 miles) of railway and 275 stations, and carries three million passengers per day.

AIR TRAVEL

The UK commercial aviation industry has experienced phenomenal growth since its early days in the mid-20th century. The

▼ Today, nearly 90 per cent of UK citizens aged between 15 and 34 own a mobile phone. Many use them for texting as much as for speaking.

number of passengers using UK airports rose from three million in 1953 to 200 million in 2003. British Airways, the UK's biggest airline, operates the world's largest network of flights, travelling to over 550 destinations in nearly 90 countries around the world. London's main airports, Heathrow and Gatwick, are among the world's busiest. In 2003, 63 million passengers used Heathrow, and 30 million passed through Gatwick.

TELECOMMUNICATIONS

The UK has one of the most advanced telecommunications systems in the world. In the 1990s and 2000s, the largest telephone service provider, British Telecom, faced increasing competition from other providers. The service evolved rapidly in the 1990s with advances in mobile telephony and the development of email, the Internet and wireless technology. By the end of 2004, there were over 60 million mobile phones in the UK, and about 2.5 million subscribers to the latest generation of mobiles, 3G. 3G mobiles can carry a lot more information, and are therefore useful for applications other than voice communication, such as TV, computer and email.

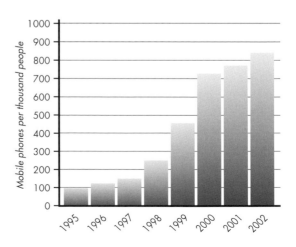

▲ Mobile phone use, 1995-2002

◀ A row of terraced houses with satellite dishes. Satellite television companies have grabbed an ever-larger share of UK TV audiences, largely because of their exclusive broadcasts of popular sports and movies.

The new technologies have been taken up at a startling rate. By the end of 2004, six million (or nearly 30 per cent) of British homes were connected to broadband, an increase of 90 per cent on 2003. By March 2005, 62 per cent of UK homes had digital TV, and consumers had a choice of over 370 TV channels. These developments are affecting the way people live with increasing numbers using the technology to work and shop from home.

 Did you know?

The UK has 148 civil airfields, 13 of which can handle more than a million passengers each.

Transport & communications data

- Total roads: 392,931 km/244,163 miles
- Total paved roads: 392,931 km/244,163 miles
- Total unpaved roads: 0 km/0 miles
- Total railways: 17,274 km/10,734 miles
- Major airports: 334
- Cars per 1,000 people: 384
- Mobile phones per 1,000 people: 841
- Personal computers per 1,000 people: 406
- Internet users per 1,000 people: 423

Source: World Bank and CIA World Factbook

Focus on: The Press

More people read newspapers in the UK than in almost any other developed nation. Around 60 per cent of adult citizens read a daily paper and more than 65 per cent buy a Sunday paper. To service this appetite, the UK has a large and diverse range of newspapers, with 10 morning dailies and nine Sunday papers published nationally. These range from 'quality' newspapers focusing on news and current affairs to the 'tabloids', which offer a mix of news, gossip and entertainment. There are also around 1,400 regional and local papers and more than 6,500 magazines.

CHAPTER 10

Education and Health

Education is vital in a developed economy such as the UK, which depends on a regular influx of educated professionals and skilled workers. The UK has one of the world's highest university graduation rates, with 36 per cent of the population achieving a first degree. It also has two world-renowned universities – Oxford and Cambridge.

SCHOOLS

All children in the UK receive compulsory primary and secondary education from the age of 5 up to the age of 16. Children attend primary school until 11, and then go on to secondary school.

▼ Pupils carry out a science experiment at a comprehensive school. Comprehensive schools admit pupils regardless of ability or social background.

Secondary schools are either publicly funded and offer free education, or they are funded by fee-paying students (known as independent schools). The vast majority of students (95 per cent) go to publicly funded schools. Most of these are 'comprehensive schools', which offer all types of secondary education and do not select their pupils. Other types of publicly funded school include specialist schools (focusing on particular subjects like the arts or sport) and grammar schools, which select all or most of their students and offer a more academic syllabus.

Since 1988, UK schools have followed the National Curriculum, designed to raise standards and set attainment targets for learning. The Curriculum has been criticized by

some for restricting teachers' freedom and for giving too little time for certain subjects. At 16, all pupils take a set of exams called GCSEs (General Certificate of Secondary Education). Pupils can then decide whether to continue their education or seek employment. About a third leave education at this stage. Those who continue can study for Advanced Level exams at 18 and apply for a place at university, or go to a college to gain vocational skills.

UNIVERSITIES

There are over 90 universities in the UK. The most famous of these are Oxford and Cambridge, both founded in the Middle Ages. Until 1998, the government paid university students a grant to help them with their costs. In the 1990s universities faced a funding crisis and the government replaced the grant with a loan to be repaid after graduation. Students were also asked to pay a proportion of their tuition fees. In the early 2000s, universities were still in financial difficulties and several were forced to close down departments. A new law was passed in 2004 introducing 'top-up fees', allowing universities to set their own tuition fees up to a cap of £3,000 per year. Some

felt that this would burden students with too much debt and dissuade many from higher education. The impact remains to be seen.

▼ The Bridge of Sighs is one of Oxford University's most famous landmarks. It joins two sections of Hertford College, whose former students include the writers John Donne, Jonathan Swift and Evelyn Waugh.

Did you know?

In 1960–1, women made up only a quarter of full-time university students in the UK. By 2002–3, 54 per cent of university undergraduates were female.

Education and health

- Life expectancy at birth male: 75.2
- Life expectancy at birth female: 80.1
- Infant mortality rate per 1,000: 5
- Under five mortality rate per 1,000: 6
- Physicians per 1,000 people: 2.1
- Health expenditure as % of GDP: 7.7
- Education expenditure as % of GDP: 4.7
- Primary net enrolment: 100%
- Pupil-teacher ratio, primary: 17.2
- Adult literacy as % age 15+: 99.0

Source: United Nations Agencies and World Bank

HEALTH

Like most developed countries, the UK has enjoyed substantial gains in the health of its population over the past 40 years. In 2003, life expectancy at birth in the UK was 77.6 years, almost eight years higher than it was in 1960, and about 0.7 years higher than average for an economically developed country. The infant mortality rate in the UK in 2003 was 5.3 deaths per 1,000 live births – lower than most developed countries, though higher than the EU average. By contrast, in 2004 the US infant mortality rate had risen to 7 per 1,000 live births.

There has been a sharp decline in the number of adult smokers in the UK. In 2003, 26 per cent of the adult population smoked compared to 40 per cent in 1978. However, there has also been a dramatic rise in obesity. Today, around 20 per cent of the UK population is obese, three times as many as in 1983. This is already leading to increases in health problems such as diabetes, asthma and heart disease. The government has responded to this development with various steps. For example, food manufacturers have been urged to reduce levels of sugar and salt in their products, and schools are to provide healthier meals and more physical exercise for their pupils.

THE NATIONAL HEALTH SERVICE

In 1948, a National Health Service (NHS) was established in the UK. It provided free medical care for all British citizens regardless of their income, paid for out of taxation. However, the NHS of today is quite different from the vision of its founders. The service now charges for items such as prescriptions, dentures and eyeglasses. Furthermore, since 1990 the NHS has undergone various reforms by governments concerned about its rising costs and inefficiency.

In the 1990s, the Conservative government tried to increase efficiency by introducing an internal market whereby hospitals were turned into trusts and given the power to determine how they spent government funds. Many GPs (general practitioners) were given budgets to buy health care from these trusts in a scheme called GP fund holding. This system was criticized for causing a 'two-tier' health service, with GP fund holders able to obtain treatment quicker than non-fund holders.

◄ The government-sponsored five-a-day campaign encourages people to eat at least five portions of fruit and vegetables every day. As part of the national campaign, all four to six year olds are entitled to a free piece of fruit or vegetable each school day.

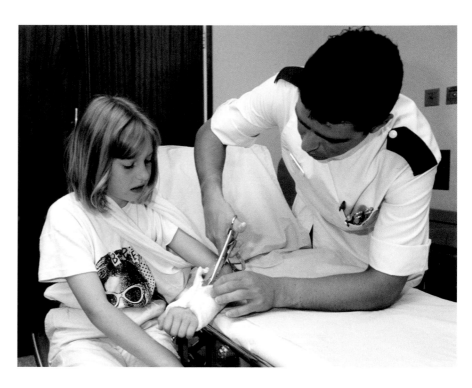

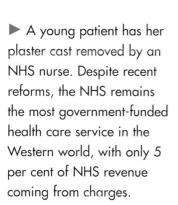
► A young patient has her plaster cast removed by an NHS nurse. Despite recent reforms, the NHS remains the most government-funded health care service in the Western world, with only 5 per cent of NHS revenue coming from charges.

Starting in 1998, the Labour government abolished the internal market and began introducing a series of new reforms. These included targets for increasing the numbers of hospitals, doctors and nurses, and reducing hospital waiting lists. They also reorganized the NHS structure, giving locally based organizations called Primary Care Trusts the power to run NHS services in their area. In

2000, the government also pledged to increase public spending on health by seven per cent per year for five years, starting in 2002, to bring it into line with other European countries. The additional funding has had mixed results. Waiting lists fell from 1.16 million in 1997 to 850,000 in September 2004. However, the UK continues to have one of the highest death rates in Europe for the 'superbug' MRSA, cancer and heart disease. As part of the government's plan to reduce NHS waiting lists, some NHS trusts have set up agreements with private healthcare providers to offer NHS patients treatment in a private hospital at no charge to the patient. Some politicians and health professionals fear that this may lead to an increasing privatization of the NHS.

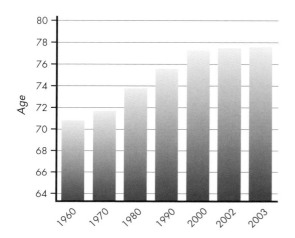
▲ Life expectancy at birth 1960-2003

Did you know?

The NHS is the largest organization in Europe, employing around 1.2 million staff and with an annual budget of about £48 billion ($85 billion).

CHAPTER 11

Culture and Religion

The UK is a country of diverse cultures and traditions. Although English culture tends to dominate, each region of the UK – Wales, Scotland and Northern Ireland – maintains its own unique customs, cuisine and festivals. Since the 1950s, immigrants from the UK's former colonies have brought Afro-Caribbean and Asian cultures to the UK.

THE ARTS

Over the centuries the UK has produced many fine artists, writers and musicians who have made their mark around the globe. The plays of William Shakespeare have enriched the English language and are performed in every part of the world. The 18th century English writers Daniel Defoe and Samuel Richardson pioneered the novel, which was taken to new heights by authors such as Jane Austen, Charles Dickens and the Brontë sisters. The poet Geoffrey Chaucer brought an earthy realism to depictions of medieval life, while William Wordsworth (1770–1850) tried to bring poetic language closer to natural speech. The English landscape painter, JMW Turner, well known for his dramatic treatment of natural light, influenced the development of impressionist painters such as Pissarro, Monet and Sisley. The writer J K Rowling thrilled a whole generation of children with her Harry Potter adventures.

In the 20th century, the UK's main contributions to world culture have been in the fields of popular music, fashion and film. In the 1960s, the Beatles and the Rolling Stones were the first British bands to win international followings, while London became known as a leader of fashion with the brightly coloured outfits being sold

◄ The Beatles arrive in the USA on one of their sell-out tours. In August 1965, the Liverpudlian band played before a record-breaking 55,600 people at New York's Shea Stadium.

in Carnaby Street and the King's Road. Since the 1960s, British film-makers such as Ken Loach and Mike Leigh have gained international respect for their portrayals of ordinary British life in movies such as *Kes* (1969) and *Life is Sweet* (1990).

FOOD AND DRINK

A traditional British meal consists of meat accompanied by potatoes and one (or more) other vegetable. Perhaps the most famous British dish is roast beef and Yorkshire pudding. Other favourites include shepherd's pie, fish and chips and (originating in the south-west) Cornish pasties and scones with clotted cream. The most popular hot drink is tea. Adults also enjoy drinking beer in pubs (public houses). Bars selling wine are also increasingly popular among city-dwellers. Since the 1950s, British cuisine has changed, due to foreign influences. Popular meals today include pizzas, hamburgers, and Chinese and Indian food.

Focus on: The Edinburgh Fringe

Every year in late summer, the city of Edinburgh hosts an international arts festival. Alongside the official festival, there is a 'Fringe' festival which offers opportunities to all performers and consequently tends to attract more unconventional acts. The Edinburgh Fringe includes a mix of theatre, comedy and music. It began when too many performers turned up to the first Edinburgh Festival in 1947, and those excluded formed their own alternative festival. In 2005, the Fringe presented almost 27,000 performances of 1,800 shows, and sold 1.25 million tickets.

▼ Every year at the Fringe, street performers entertain festivalgoers on Edinburgh's Royal Mile.

CHRISTIAN WORSHIP

Since Henry VIII's split with the Roman Catholic Church in the 16th century, the UK has officially been a Protestant country. The national Churches in the UK are the Church of England (or Anglican Church) and the Church of Scotland (or Presbyterian Church). The Churches in Wales and Northern Ireland are part of the Anglican Communion, meaning that they recognize the authority of the Anglican Church.

Further splits in the Church of England in the 17th century led to the founding of 'Nonconformist' Churches such as the Baptists and Congregationalists, who desired simpler forms of worship. The Methodist Church was founded in the 18th century as part of a religious revival centred on the industrial northeast, where it remains strong. The Presbyterian Church of Wales, closely linked with Welsh culture and language, was founded in the 18th century and is still a significant religious body in that region.

There are around 49.5 million Christians in the UK, including 5.6 million Catholics. This represents almost 83 per cent of the population. However, very few British Christians actually attend church except for baptisms, weddings and funerals. Around a million people attend Anglican churches each Sunday.

OTHER RELIGIOUS GROUPS

Although the official religion of the UK is Protestantism, it is a country of religious freedom, and people are allowed to practise whatever faith they like without interference from the state. Catholics have continued living in the UK since the Reformation, Jews have settled in the UK since the 17th century, and there has been a growth in other non-Christian communities since the immigration of the 1950s. There are currently around 1,589,000 Muslims, 558,000 Hindus, 336,000 Sikhs, 267,000 Jews and 149,000 Buddhists living in the UK.

◄ A bride and groom are showered with confetti at a traditional church wedding in Cllitheroe, Lancashire. Around a third of all weddings in Britain are performed in an Anglican church.

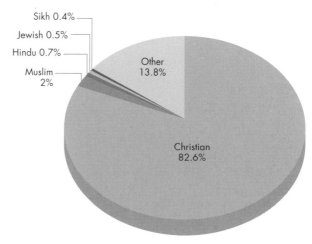 A congregation gathers at a British mosque in Preston, Lancashire, for Friday prayers. Every year, around 20,000 British Muslims travel to Mecca for the Hajj (an annual pilgrimage).

RELIGIOUS TENSIONS

Because of the UK's tradition of tolerance, the country has suffered relatively little religious tension. One of the few places where religion and politics are still entwined is Northern Ireland. Here, the Protestant majority wish to maintain the union with the UK, while the Roman Catholic minority support union with Ireland. This long-running conflict blew up into 30 years of violent troubles, beginning in 1969 (see page 25).

Another more recent source of tension has emerged with the rise of militant fundamentalists within the Muslim community,

partly inflamed by the UK's role in the war against Iraq. On 7 July 2005 a group of these Islamists set off bombs in central London killing 56 people. A further set of attacks was attempted two weeks later, but failed. Since then the government has acted to ban certain extremist organizations and deport a number of radical preachers.

 Did you know?

The UK has one of the largest Muslim communities in Western Europe, and over 600 mosques and prayer centres. One of the most important Muslim institutions in the Western world is the Central Mosque in London.

Sikh 0.4%
Jewish 0.5%
Hindu 0.7%
Muslim 2%
Other 13.8%
Christian 82.6%

▲ The United Kingdom's major religions

CHAPTER 12

Leisure and Tourism

People in the UK work an average of 44.8 hours per week, and receive an average of between four and five weeks of holiday per year. In addition, they have days off around the major festivals of Christmas, New Year and Easter, and there are three extra 'bank holidays' in May and August.

LEISURE PURSUITS

The most popular leisure activities in the UK are watching television or listening to music or the radio. An average of three hours per day are spent watching TV. While 99 per cent of British people watch television, just 65 per cent read books.

Cinema is another favourite pastime. There were 171 million visits to UK cinemas in 2004, making the UK second highest in Europe, after France, for cinema attendances. Theatres, museums and art galleries are also well attended, with visits from 24 per cent of the population.

KEEPING ACTIVE

The British are also great lovers of sport – both watching and playing it. Around 59 per cent of adults take part in some regular sport, exercise or outdoor pursuit. The most popular are walking, swimming, aerobic exercise, yoga, cycling and snooker or pool. Nearly 10 per cent of the population are members of health clubs, leisure centres or gyms. Fishing, climbing, sailing and bird watching are also common outdoor pursuits. Another favourite activity is gardening – about half the families in the UK have a garden.

The most popular spectator sport is football. Every Saturday during the football season, thousands of fans attend matches in every town and city in the country. Several of the top

▼ Rambling is a highly popular activity in the UK. The Ramblers' Association has almost 140,000 members in England, Scotland and Wales.

◀ Players from Scotland's two biggest football teams, Celtic (green and white hoops) and Rangers, tussle for the ball.

British football clubs, such as Manchester United and Liverpool are known worldwide.

Other popular spectator sports include rugby, cricket, track and field athletics and horse racing. Tennis becomes briefly popular for two weeks each summer during the Wimbledon Championships.

Since the 1990s, there has been a decline in sport in British schools. The increased emphasis on teaching children literacy and numeracy has meant less time for physical education and sport. School playing fields have been sold off to local councils and private developers. The government has tried to reverse this trend by developing specialist sports schools, bringing coaching specialists into schools, and encouraging high-profile sports stars to make school visits. The status of sport is likely to grow in UK schools, with London having been awarded the 2012 Olympic Games.

Focus on: The London Marathon

The London Marathon, which takes place each year in April, is the world's largest marathon, attracting over 100,000 applications for the 20,000 available places. A further 25,000 places are reserved for charity runners. Its 26.2-mile course runs from Greenwich Park in south-east London to the Mall and Buckingham Palace. Over 375,000 spectators line the route. Each year the marathon raises around £30 million for charity.

▲ The Eden Project in Cornwall, one of the UK's top tourist attractions, aims to promote understanding of the natural world. Its domes are 'biomes', housing plants from tropical and temperate regions.

TOURISM IN THE UK

The UK tourist industry has grown dramatically in recent years, with the number of foreign visitors doubling between 1983 and 2003 from around 12 million to 24 million. The majority of tourists are from Europe, with 16 million visitors in 2003 – four times the number from North America. However, most tourist trips in the UK are made by UK residents. For example, in 2002, 167.3 million tourist visits were made to different parts of the UK by British residents – 87.3 per cent of the total.

There are about 6,400 tourist attractions in the United Kingdom, including museums, art galleries, wildlife centres, historic houses and castles, churches and cathedrals, gardens and leisure parks. In 2001, these received a total of 452 million visits. Popular attractions include (not in order of popularity): Blackpool Pleasure Beach in Lancashire, Brighton Pier, the Eden Project in Cornwall, the Lake District in Cumbria, Hadrian's Wall in Northumbria, Snowdonia in Wales, the Peak District National Park and Edinburgh Castle in Scotland.

However, by far the most popular destination for overseas tourists is London, which received 11.7 million visitors in 2003. Many come to see the capital city's world famous sights, its galleries and museums. Top attractions (based on visitor numbers) include the Tower of London, the National Gallery, the British Museum – which houses tremendous collections and wonders, including the Rosetta Stone, Egyptian sphinxes, and rare books – the London Eye (the largest observation wheel in the world), and the Tate Modern, an art museum.

In total, the UK tourist industry is worth approximately £16 billion per year – around six per cent of the gross domestic product. And it's growing – about one in five of all new jobs created in the UK since 1997 have been in the tourist industry. However, foreign tourists spend about £4.5 billion less in the UK than British tourists spend abroad.

HOLIDAYS ABROAD

Taking holidays overseas has become a lot cheaper in recent decades, with the emergence of package holidays and low-cost airlines. This has led to a huge growth in the number of Britons taking foreign holidays. UK residents made a record 41.2 million holiday trips abroad in 2003, compared to just 6.7 million foreign holidays in 1971. Almost half the trips taken in 2003 were package holidays.

Since 1994, the favourite destination for British holidaymakers has been Spain, which was the venue for 30 per cent of all UK foreign holidays in 2003. The next most popular destination was France, with 18 per cent. In fact, nine out of the ten most frequently visited countries are in the EU. The exception is the USA, which attracted five per cent of all holidays.

▲ The London Eye takes people above the London skyline, giving them spectacular views of up to 25 miles across the city and beyond, including St Paul's, the Palace of Westminster and Windsor Castle.

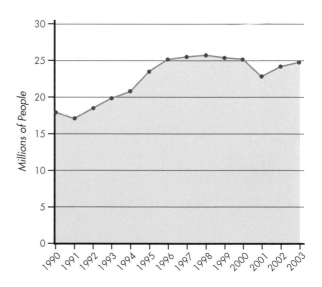

▲ Changes in international tourism, 1990-2002

Tourism in The United Kingdom

- 🗁 Tourist arrivals, millions: 24.785
- 🗁 Earnings from tourism in US$:
  30,656,000,000
- 🗁 Tourism as % foreign earnings: 7.0
- 🗁 Tourist departures, millions: 61.453
- 🗁 Expenditure on tourism in US$:
  58,602,000,384

Source: World Bank

 Did you know?

The UK is the sixth most popular holiday destination in the world, after France, Spain, USA, China and Italy.

CHAPTER 13

Environment and Conservation

There is mounting scientific evidence of the negative effect of human consumption patterns on the environment. In the UK this can be seen, for example, in the poor air quality of many British cities caused by high levels of road traffic. The UK government, under pressure from environmental activists and concerned citizens, has concluded that current lifestyles are unsustainable.

CLIMATE CHANGE

Much of the UK's economic prosperity was built on the use of fossil fuels. However, most scientists believe that the emissions of carbon dioxide and other greenhouse gases, caused by burning fossil fuels, are starting to change the world's climate. In 1997, the UK signed the Kyoto Protocol, legally binding the government to reduce the UK's greenhouse gas emissions by 12.5 per cent below 1990 levels by 2008–12. In 2000, the UK government set itself an even tougher target of cutting carbon dioxide emissions by 20 per cent below 1990 levels by 2010.

To achieve these targets, the government planned a £12 million campaign to change public attitudes and try to promote better energy efficiency at home and at work. Other measures included cutting emissions from road vehicles by encouraging the use of low-emitting cars and buses; increasing the proportion of UK electricity produced from renewable energy

▼ This zero-emissions car at Sussex University illustrates the potential for a more environmentally friendly future for British road vehicles.

sources to 10 per cent by 2010; and ensuring that new buildings are more energy efficient, for example by providing better insulation for walls and roofs to prevent heat loss. Some progress has been made: greenhouse gas emissions in 2002 were 15 per cent below 1990s levels. However, in 2005, just 3.6 per cent of UK electricity was produced from renewable sources compared to an EU average of 14 per cent.

WASTE AND RECYCLING

The environmental impact of waste can be reduced by recycling or composting as much of it as possible. Estimates suggest that as much as 60 per cent of household waste could be recycled, yet England managed just 17.7 per cent in 2003–4 – one of the lowest rates in Europe. Regional differences are marked. In 2001–2, the north-east of England managed to recycle just 62 kg (136 lb) per household per year, while households in south-eastern England averaged 222 kg (488 lb) per year. The government has set a target to increase the amount of recycled waste to 30 per cent in 2010 and 33 per cent by 2015. They plan to meet these targets by providing kerbside recycling collection to every household in the country.

POLLUTION

As an industrialized nation, pollution of air and water has been a problem in the UK since the 19th century. Since the Clean Air Acts of 1956 and 1968, which banned coal burning in urban areas, emissions of sulphur dioxide and smoke

▲ Recycled waste being collected from people's kerbsides in London. The government and the local authorities have embarked on a campaign to persuade more people to recycle more of their household waste.

 Did you know?

The UK produces well over 100 million tonnes (98 million tons) of industrial and domestic waste annually, and this quantity is growing by three per cent every year.

have fallen dramatically. In the 1980s, the UK signed international protocols to reduce emissions of nitrogen oxides that cause acid rain. Nitrogen oxides emissions in the UK fell by 44 per cent between 1990 and 2003 to 1,570 tonnes (*1545 tons*).

The UK's rivers have also suffered in the past due to discharges from industry and agriculture and sewage treatment works. However, since 1990, the water companies have spent £6 billion cleaning up Britain's rivers, and they plan to spend a further £2 billion by 2010. This effort has brought some improvements, with 65 per cent of rivers achieving good quality ratings in 2004 – 17 per cent better than in 1990.

▼ A volunteer helps to clear the River Wandle in London of rubbish. The Wandle was once a highly polluted river that has recently been cleaned up.

WILDLIFE CONSERVATION

Wildlife has suffered numerous threats in the UK over the past hundred years. Problems include habitat loss, caused, for example, by farmers draining wetlands for agriculture and allowing overgrazing on upland moors. Another threat comes from the introduction of non-native species that eat or out-compete with native species. For example, the grey squirrel, introduced in the 1800s, is thought to have caused a decline in the native red squirrel population. Pollution also damages sensitive species or ecosystems.

In recent years, the government-funded Environment Agency has worked to improve the UK's biodiversity (the range of living things in a country, region or ecological system) through Habitat Action Plans, improving 45 wildlife habitats around the country. The agency has also introduced 391 Species Action Plans to sustain and increase the populations of threatened species, including otters, water voles, southern damselflies and barn owls.

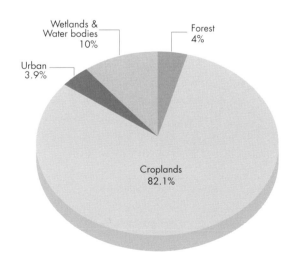

Wetlands & Water bodies 10%

Forest 4%

Urban 3.9%

Croplands 82.1%

▲ Types of habitat

Bird populations are a good indicator of the general health of a country's wildlife. The overall bird population increased by 13 per cent between 1970 and 2002, although there was a slight decrease between 2000 and 2002. Successful species include the Dartford warbler, which may have benefited from climate change because the warmer climate has expanded the area where it can breed in the UK to include more northerly areas. However, farmland species such as turtledove and skylark fell by 42 per cent between 1970 and 2002, mainly because of intensive farming, which robbed them of some of their habitat. Overgrazing and the concentrated use of fertilizers have caused a reduction in the plants and insects on which these birds feed.

► The red squirrel is one native species that has become seriously endangered, with only around 160,000 remaining, compared to over 2.5 million grey squirrels.

Environmental and conservation data

🗁 Forested area as % total land area: 4

🗁 Protected area as % total land area: 10.5

🗁 Number of protected areas: 7,191

SPECIES DIVERSITY

Category	Known species	Threatened species
Mammals	50	12
Breeding birds	229	2
Reptiles	15	n/a
Amphibians	12	n/a
Fish	427	3
Plants	1,623	13

Source: World Resources Institute

Focus on: The Wildfowl and Wetlands Trust

Wetlands have been called the kidneys of the natural environment due to their ability to clean pollutants from the water supply. Wetland environments in the UK are protected under international and national law because of their unique biodiversity. Established in 1946 by the artist and conservationist Sir Peter Scott, the Wildfowl and Wetlands Trust has campaigned to conserve and protect the UK's wetland environments. Its aim is to sustain the habitat of migratory wildfowl and to protect the rare and delicate ecosystem that brings benefits to bird and animal life.

CHAPTER 14

Future Challenges

The United Kingdom has enjoyed steady economic growth and relative social and political stability in recent years. However, it also faces a number of challenges, including regional economic disparities, inter-community tensions and environmental issues.

NORTH AND SOUTH

The UK's economic success is not felt evenly through the country. A wealth gap is growing between the prosperous south-east and the former industrial centres of the north and northeast. In some areas of the UK, especially the inner cities, there is real poverty. As the south-east has prospered, more and more young people have moved south for jobs. This rapid population growth has led to a major housing shortage and placed pressures on the transport infrastructure. The government has had some success in attracting businesses back to the north, but more needs to be done in this area to avoid increasing perceptions of a north-south divide.

TENSIONS BETWEEN COMMUNITIES

The Northern Ireland peace process received a boost in July 2005 when the IRA announced the end of its armed struggle. Hopes were raised that the IRA would decommission its weapons and that the Northern Ireland Assembly would be restored. However, the long history of the struggle between loyalists and republicans in this region suggests that full disarmament and restoration will be difficult to achieve.

The racist attitudes suffered by immigrants in the 1970s have declined, although there are signs that a dislike of foreigners is returning in some cities in the north-west of England where the far-right British National Party (BNP) has made gains. The BNP exploited public fears about the country being swamped by immigrants and asylum seekers. If such attitudes grow, it may start to erode the UK's reputation as a liberal and tolerant society.

◀ A new business park being built in Stafford in the North Midlands – part of efforts to bridge the north-south economic divide by encouraging business and creating jobs in areas other than the south-east. The countryside is changing dramatically as more business parks are built.

ENVIRONMENTAL CHALLENGES

The UK is engaged in a process of transition from an old-style energy-inefficient, fossil-fuel-based economy to one based on principles of sustainable development. This transition is a long-term project and its success will depend on changing public attitudes as much as government action. The most urgent challenge is to find alternative, cleaner energy sources that will meet UK domestic and industrial needs.

EUROPE

One of the UK's major foreign policy challenges is to decide on its relationship with Europe. The issue of EU membership has divided the British people for many years. Britain is a fiercely proud and independent nation with a rich history and a distinctive culture. The challenge for the UK is to retain its unique character whilst also enjoying the economic and political benefits of being part of Europe.

▲ United we stand: Londoners observe a two-minute silence for the victims of the 7 July 2005 London bombings and in defiance of those who sought to destroy their way of life.

Today, the United Kingdom continues to be one of the world's leading industrial nations. Its historical links with countries all over the world have given the UK both a strong voice in world affairs and a richly diverse culture. The UK is therefore uniquely placed to benefit from the increasingly global nature of business and society. However, the UK's elevated status on the world stage can also bring challenges such as war and terrorism. As a modern, industrialized nation it must take its share of responsibility for pollution and the growing rich-poor divide. Closer to home, the British people must also find ways of balancing economic success with a healthy, sustainable lifestyle.

Timeline

c. 6500 BC Formation of the island of Great Britain.

55 BC Julius Caesar invades Britain.

AD 43–410 Period of the Roman occupation of Britain.

449 Angles, Saxons and Jutes begin to invade Britain.

c. 490–c. 550 Anglo-Saxon kingdoms established.

787 Viking raids begin.

802 Egbert of Wessex becomes king of all England.

871–99 Alfred the Great, King of Wessex, defends England against the Vikings.

1066 William, Duke of Normandy, defeats Harold II at Hastings, and becomes king of England.

1138–1153 Civil war in England.

1154 Henry II (Henry of Anjou) becomes the first Plantagenet king.

1215 King John signs the Magna Carta.

1337–1453 England fights the Hundred Years' War with France.

1348–51 The Black Death wipes out a third of Britain's population.

1455–1485 The Wars of the Roses.

1485 Henry VII becomes the first Tudor monarch.

1534 Henry VIII passes the Act of Supremacy, establishing himself as leader of the English Church.

1536–43 Wales is annexed to England.

1558–1603 Reign of Queen Elizabeth I.

1588 England defeats the Spanish Armada.

1605 The Gunpowder Plot to blow up Parliament is foiled.

1642–9 The English Civil War is fought between supporters of King Charles I and Parliament.

1649–1660 The Commonwealth, established by Oliver Cromwell, briefly replaces the monarchy.

1660 Restoration of the monarchy under Charles II.

1688–9 The defeat of James II and accession of William I ends a further threat to English Protestantism.

1707 The Act of Union joins England and Scotland and establishes the nation of Great Britain.

1756–1763 Britain fights the Seven Years' War with France, establishing its supremacy in India and North America.

1783 Britain loses the American War of Independence.

1801 Ireland is annexed to Britain to form the United Kingdom.

1805 Napoléon's fleet is defeated by Nelson at the Battle of Trafalgar.

1815 Napoléon is defeated by Wellington at the Battle of Waterloo.

1837–1901 Reign of Queen Victoria.

1914–18 World War I.

1921 The partition of Ireland. Ulster remains part of the UK.

1939–45 World War II. UK cities are heavily bombed in the Blitz.

1948 The British government establishes the National Health Service.

1968-9 The Troubles begin in Northern Ireland.

1973 The UK joins the EEC.

1975 The first oil is brought ashore from the North Sea.

1982 The UK fights and wins the Falklands War against Argentina.

1999 Powers are devolved from the UK government to regional assemblies.

2001–2 British involvement in military attacks against Afghanistan.

2003 British forces take part in the war against Iraq.

2005 Suicide bombers blow themselves up in London, killing 56 people.

Glossary

Anglican Communion The Churches in communion with, and recognizing the authority of, the Church of England.

Annexed Taken over.

Asylum seekers People who request permission to live in another state because they face repression in their own country.

Balance of trade The difference between the value of imports and exports of a country over a fixed period.

Biodiversity The variety of living things found in a particular environment. A high level of biodiversity is beneficial to an environment because it makes it more resistant to external activities such as natural or human-made disasters.

Biomass Plant and animal material used as a source of food.

Carbon dioxide emissions Discharges of the gas carbon dioxide (CO_2), produced whenever fuel is burned. CO_2 is one of the main 'greenhouse gases' which contribute to global warming.

Cold War The conflict between the USA and the Soviet Union and their allies which lasted from 1945 to 1990.

Common Agricultural Policy (CAP) The EU's agricultural policy, intended to provide stable markets and incomes for European farmers.

Constituency One of the areas into which a country is divided for election purposes.

Constitution A set of rules by which a country is governed.

Constitutional monarchy A political system in which the head of state is a monarch ruling to the extent allowed by a constitution.

Devolve To transfer power from central government to regional governments.

Ecosystem A group of interdependent plants and animals together with the environment they inhabit and depend on.

Electoral system The system under which elections are held in a particular country.

European Union (EU) An economic and political alliance of European nations.

Feudalism The system that existed in medieval Europe in which barons were given land by the king in exchange for military service.

Fossil fuels Any carbon-containing fuel, such as coal, natural gas and oil.

Glaciers Large bodies of slowly moving ice and compacted snow.

Global warming The gradual increase in the Earth's average temperature probably caused by the burning of fossil fuels such as oil.

Gross domestic product The total value of goods and services produced by a nation.

Gross national product The total value of goods and services produced by a nation, including goods and services produced abroad.

Infrastructure The large-scale public systems, services and equipment needed for a country to function, including roads and telecommunications

Islamist An extremist Muslim who wishes to enforce Islamic law on society.

Legislation Laws

Lingua franca A language used between people who have no other language in common.

National Curriculum The framework for teaching and learning across a range of subjects to be followed by all school-age pupils in the UK.

Nationalize To transfer a business or industry from private ownership to government control.

North Atlantic Treaty Organization (NATO) A military alliance of 20 nations in North America and Europe, established in 1949 during the Cold War with the USSR and its allies.

Nuclear energy The energy released by nuclear fission (the splitting of an atomic nucleus into smaller nuclei).

Parliament The UK's legislative body where bills are debated and passed into law.

Partition Division.

Precipitation Rain, snow or hail.

Privatize To transfer a business or industry from government control to private ownership.

Protestant Reformation The 16th century movement in Europe that led to the development of Protestant Churches.

Sovereignty Supreme authority over a state.

Subsidies Grants from a government to businesses or organizations to help them function.

Tabloids Small-format newspapers with an emphasis on sensational stories.

United Nations (UN) An organization of nations, formed in 1945, to promote peace, security, and international cooperation.

Wetland A marsh, swamp or other area of land where the soil near the surface is saturated with water.

Further Information

BOOKS TO READ

Changing Face of the United Kingdom
Rob Bowden
(Hodder Wayland, 2004)

Countries of the World: United Kingdom
Rob Bowden
(Evans Publishing, 2002)

Visual Geography Series: United Kingdom in Pictures
Kumari Campbell
(Lerner Publications, 2004)

Focus on Europe: Britain and the British
Anita Ganeri
(Franklin Watts, 2001)

Country File: Great Britain
C. Oliver
(Franklin Watts, 2001)

Geography 21: United Kingdom
Simon Ross
(HarperCollins, 1998)

A Citizen's Guide to: Governing the UK
Ivan Minnis
(Heinemann Library, 2002)

USEFUL WEBSITES

http://www.statistics.gov.uk/
Statistics on every aspect of UK life, including the population, economy, health, transport and education.

http://www.direct.gov.uk/
Information about the UK government.

http://news.bbc.co.uk/1/hi/world/europe/country_profiles/1038758.stm
A BBC website offering a comprehensive country profile of the UK.

http://www.bbc.co.uk/history/timelines/britain/
A BBC website offering a timeline of British history.

http://www.channel4.com/history
A Channel 4 television website offering features on British history.

http://www.metoffice.com/climate/uk/
Information and statistics on the UK climate from the Met Office.

http://www.environment-agency.gov.uk
Information on measures to protect and improve the environment.

http://www.number_10.gov.uk/
The website of the office of the British Prime Minister.

http://www.thecommonwealth.org/
The website of the Commonwealth which includes a link to the Young Person's Commonwealth site.

Index

About the author

Alex Woolf studied History and Government at Essex University. He has spent over ten years as an editor and writer of children's books on history, geography and social issues. He lives with his wife and son in Southgate, North London.